# YOU SHOULD MEET

# Women Who Launched the Computer Age

by Laurie Calkhoven
illustrated by Alyssa Petersen

Ready-to-Read

Simon Spotlight
New York   London   Toronto   Sydney   New Delhi

SIMON SPOTLIGHT
An imprint of Simon & Schuster Children's Publishing Division
1230 Avenue of the Americas, New York, New York 10020
This Simon Spotlight edition September 2016
Text copyright © 2016 by Simon & Schuster, Inc.
Illustrations copyright © 2016 by Alyssa Petersen
All rights reserved, including the right of reproduction in whole or in part in any form.
SIMON SPOTLIGHT, READY-TO-READ, and colophon are registered trademarks
of Simon & Schuster, Inc. • For information about special discounts for bulk purchases, please contact
Simon & Schuster Special Sales at 1-866-506-1949 or business@simonandschuster.com.
Manufactured in the United States of America 0521 LAK
6 8 10 9 7 5
Library of Congress Cataloging-in-Publication Data:
Names: Calkhoven, Laurie. | Petersen, Alyssa, illustrator.
Title: The women who launched the computer age / by Laurie Calkhoven;
illustrated by Alyssa Petersen.
Description: New York : Simon Spotlight, [2016]
Series: You should meet | Series: Ready-to-read | Audience: Age 6–8.
Identifiers: LCCN 2016021574 | ISBN 9781481470476 | ISBN 9781481470483 | ISBN 9781481470469
Subjects: LCSH: Women computer scientists—United States—Biography—Juvenile literature.
Computer scientists—United States—Biography—Juvenile literature. | Women computer
programmers—United States—Biography—Juvenile literature. | Computer
programmers—United States—Biography—Juvenile literature. ENIAC
(Computer)—History—Juvenile literature. Computer industry—
United States—History—Juvenile literature.
Classification: LCC QA76.2.A2 C35 2016 | DDC 004.092 [B]—dc23
LC record available at https://lccn.loc.gov/2016021574

# CONTENTS

# The World before Computers

Where would we be without computers? Today a computer can fit into your pocket or even on your wrist. You can watch a video or get the answer to a question in seconds. That's because computers run *programs*, lists of instructions that tell them what to do. Programs tell computers how to do everything, from searching the Internet, to giving directions, to playing games. But just like the physical computer had to be invented, so did the language of programming. This is the story of one of the very first computers and the people who programmed it.

The United States Army built a computer called ENIAC (pronounced "EE-nee-ack") to help the US fight against its enemies in World War II. "ENIAC" stands for "Electronic Numerical Integrator and Computer."

ENIAC was the very first computer that could do more than one type of mathematical equation at a time. Depending on how information flowed through the computer, it could give the answers to many different, really difficult math problems. In one second, ENIAC could execute 5,000 additions, 357 multiplications, and 38 divisions.

The ENIAC engineers knew they had built an

amazing machine, but getting it to do what they wanted was another challenge. They didn't know it yet, but what they needed were "computer programs" and "computer programmers."

A group of smart women were chosen to make ENIAC work. They had to figure out how to make the information flow through the computer to get the answers they wanted. In short, they were the very first computer programmers.

You should meet the women who helped launch the computer age. You should meet the **women who programmed ENIAC!**

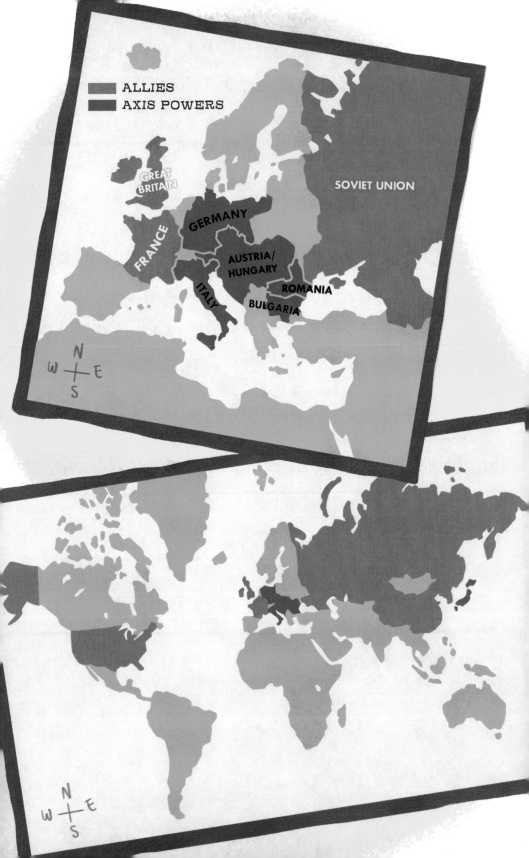

# Chapter 1
## World at War

In the early 1940s, the world was at war. Almost every country in the world took part in World War II. The United States, Great Britain, the Soviet Union, China, and other countries were on one side of the War. They were called the *Allies*. Germany, Japan, and the countries that supported them, the *Axis powers*, were on the other side. The war between the Allied countries and the Axis powers lasted for many years.

The United States military used complicated weapons to fight the war. Their weapons had to be set just right so that missiles would land in exactly the right spot once they were fired. Setting the weapons required a lot of mathematical calculations.

With the help of adding machines, it took a human being thirty to forty hours to do the math for each target. Adding machines could do only one calculation at

a time and thousands of calculations had to be done.

The army needed lots of people who were good at math to do these problems. They called these mathematicians "computers." So when somebody said, "We need a computer to do this job," they were referring to a *person*, not a machine!

With men away fighting the war overseas, the military hired women to be the mathematicians. The military put out an ad for female math majors in colleges around the country to come to Philadelphia to be "computers."

At that time, most women who had college degrees in mathematics became teachers. Other mathematics jobs in science or research usually went to men. Being a "computer" was an interesting new opportunity for women who were good at math.

# Chapter 2
## Meet the Human Computers

Jean Jennings grew up on a farm in Missouri. She was a star pitcher and as a child, she was the only girl on her school softball team. She majored in math in college, but teaching wasn't for her. She wanted to see the world and have adventures. When Jean read that the military needed math majors, she applied for the job. When she got it, she hopped on a train to Philadelphia.

Kay McNulty was born in Ireland. She moved to the United States with her family when she was three. At college, Kay became friends with another math major, Frances Bilas. When Kay

saw the ad for math majors, she called Frances.

Together, Kay and Frances went on a job interview, and one week later they were hired.

Ruth Lichterman was from New York City. She studied mathematics at Hunter College. Like the others, she wanted to help the United States win the war. So she went to Philadelphia to be a **human computer.**

Betty Snyder was from Philadelphia. She went to college to major in math. One of her college professors, like many other people at the time, believed mathematics was something only men should study. Betty decided to change her major to journalism, but she still loved math. When the army needed human computers, she signed up.

Marlyn Wescoff never took a mathematics class in college. But she was extremely smart and knew how to use an adding machine, so she was hired to be a computer too.

Marlyn got math lessons on the job. "This was wonderful, strange, difficult, and exciting," she said.

While these women were calculating how to set weapons, they had no idea what they were going to be asked to do next.

# Chapter 3
## Top Secret!

By this time, World War II had been going on for many years. Everyone wanted it to end. The military thought that doing calculations faster might help them win the war.

Engineers John W. Mauchly and John Presper Eckert Jr. built a high-speed general-use computer to do calculations in seconds, not hours. That computer was ENIAC. (A *general-use computer* is one that, given the correct application, should be able to perform most common computing tasks.)

ENIAC was enormous—eight feet high and eighty feet long! It took up a whole room! It had more than six thousand switches and almost eighteen thousand vacuum tubes. If it was used correctly, ENIAC could do long, hard math problems in seconds. ENIAC was a thousand times faster than the human computers and adding machines that came before it.

But to solve a math problem, ENIAC had to be told *how* to solve it. That meant that all of its cables and switches had to be arranged in a specific pattern. Each problem required the cables to be set in a different sequence and no one knew ahead of time what those patterns were.

The military turned to its human computers for help.

Jean Jennings, Kay McNulty, Frances Bilas, Ruth Lichterman, Betty Snyder, and Marlyn Wescoff were chosen to work on this new project. They were going to make ENIAC work.

The women were told ENIAC was top secret. They couldn't even tell their parents that they were working on it.

The women worked together, lived together, and ate together while they were being trained to work on ENIAC. It was a good thing they all got along and became friends!

"We had a wonderful time with each other," Jean said.

After six weeks of training, the women were left alone to figure out how ENIAC worked. The engineers helped them when they could, but they had moved on to other projects. The women discovered that if they put a cable in a certain place, ENIAC would do one thing, and if they put the cable in a different place, it would do another. There were no books they could read. No classes to teach them. They had to figure it out on the job.

Then they had to make ENIAC do math. First they broke down long, complicated math problems into simple steps. Then they made charts and diagrams for each step. Then they used their charts to set up the steps on ENIAC. They moved cables and flipped switches to make the machine perform the steps. By setting up the cables in the right pattern, they were programming the computer. If programmed just right, ENIAC would solve the math problem correctly and fast.

There were thousands of cables and switches to arrange. The women realized that they could save time by reusing steps of one program in another. They were getting better at programming.

The women soon knew more about ENIAC than the men who had designed it. They programmed the computer to do a series of top secret math problems for the military.

On September 2, 1945, World War II officially ended. The United States and the other Allied powers had won without the help of ENIAC, but it was still an important invention. It remained a secret until February 1946, when the army and the men who had designed the computer decided it was time to show it to the world.

They gave the women a specific math problem they wanted them to program ENIAC to solve. The women had two weeks to create the new program. After all the time and money that had gone into creating this computer, ENIAC had to succeed in its first public showing. It was all up to these six women!

# Chapter 4
## The Amazing ENIAC

Here is the task the women of ENIAC were given: They had to design a program that showed how ENIAC could pinpoint exactly where a missile would land.

And their program had to be perfect. One mistake, and the world would think ENIAC was a failure.

The women broke up into three teams.

Jean and Betty took on the job of programming ENIAC. Marlyn and Ruth helped by doing the math by hand to check every step. Kay and Frances thought up ways to reuse steps in the program to save time.

The women worked hard for two weeks. The night before ENIAC's big presentation, they were still checking and fixing their program.

There was one glitch that they couldn't fix.

The ENIAC program wouldn't stop computing when the missile hit its target. Instead, the program was telling the missile to keep traveling all the way to the center of the earth. Of course this could never happen in real life—a missile would blow up when it hit its target—but in the simulation, this error made it look like ENIAC didn't work.

Jean and Betty couldn't figure out where they'd gone wrong. They went to bed believing that ENIAC was going to fail in front of the whole world.

Betty woke up in the middle of the night and suddenly knew the answer. She rushed to ENIAC early the next morning and flipped one more switch. The program worked!

Jean said Betty solved more problems in her sleep than other people did awake!

On February 14, 1946, ENIAC was shown to the world. It solved math problems that would have taken a human hours to solve in seconds. ENIAC made news all over the globe.

That night, after the presentation, there was a big dinner to celebrate ENIAC's success. But none of the women who had programmed ENIAC were invited.

The dinner honored the men who'd built the machine. No one talked about the women who programmed it. The women knew that programming the first general-use computer was as important as building it. The women of ENIAC were pioneers in the computer age, but their names were lost to history.

# Chapter 5
## Trailblazers

The women of ENIAC went on to work at
other computer jobs. They got married.
They had children. They lived their
lives. But no one remembered that they
had programmed the first general-use
computer. Many of the tools they came up
with are still used in programming today.
But the six women were the forgotten
trailblazers of the computer age.

Then in 1985, almost forty years later,
a college student named Kathy Kleiman
was working on a paper about women in
computing.

She saw pictures of ENIAC with men and women standing in front of it. The captions for the pictures named only the men. Kathy asked who the women were and was told they were models hired to show off the computer. That didn't sound right to her.

Kathy Kleiman searched for the truth. She tracked down the women in the pictures and learned what they had done.

Kathy wanted everyone to know how important the women of ENIAC were. She wrote about them and shared their story.

Since then the women who programmed ENIAC have gone on to win many awards. They have been written about in books and magazines and have appeared on TV news shows. Kathy even made a documentary about their work.

Every time you talk on a cell phone, type on a computer, or play a video game, you are running a computer program. You have the women of ENIAC to thank for making that possible.

Those six women were the first people to learn how to program a computer to make those kinds of tasks fast and easy. They laid the foundation for every electronic device in use today—from cell phones to laptop computers to rockets launched into outerspace.

The world should remember how important those six bright women were. Now that you've met them, don't you agree?

**BUT WAIT . . .**

**THERE'S MORE!**

Now that you know a little bit about ENIAC, turn the page to learn more about computer programming, and read some fun facts about computers, cell phones, and keyboards.

# The History of Programming

Computers are a modern invention, but people have tried to make math easier for thousands of years. The Ishango Bone may be considered one of the first counting tools. It's believed that people in central Africa carved and

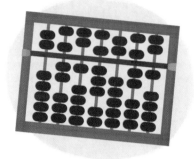

**Abacus**

used the bone to keep track of numbers. The abacus, invented by the Chinese twenty-five hundred years ago, helped people add and subtract big numbers.

Joseph-Marie Jacquard, born in France, was the first person to "talk" to a machine. In 1801, he invented a *loom*, a machine that weaves yarn or thread to make fabric, that could follow instructions. To tell the loom what to do, Jacquard made punch cards. If there was a hole in a certain place on the card, the machine moved in a certain way. We call this "machine code." Once Jacquard put the cards in the loom and set it in motion, his work was done. The machine followed the code and wove the cloth exactly the way Jacquard wanted!

In the 1840s in Britain, Ada Lovelace wrote the first computer

**Loom**

program for a non-electronic computer called the Analytical Engine—it used lots of gears to do different types of math. Lovelace wrote a set of instructions for the Analytical Engine.

The machine would be able to follow the instructions Ms. Lovelace had written, and solve math problems on its own.

Analytical Engine

A century later electronic computers such as ENIAC were invented. Instead of using gears to do math, tiny particles called electrons flowed through tubes in the computer. The programmers told the computer what type of math it should do by controlling where the electrons went.

Over the years, wires and tubes were replaced by tiny computer chips. To tell the electrons how to flow, programmers used Ada Lovelace's idea. They gave the computer instructions. They invented a language called FORTRAN, short for FORmula TRANslation, that the computer could follow. Programmers wrote the instructions in FORTRAN, and the computer did the rest!

FORTRAN was just about teaching computers math, but today computers can do much more than math. That's because programmers have written lots of instructions for them. From searching the Internet to listening to music, whenever you use a computer, you're using a program. What will computers do next?

# Zeros and Ones

Telling computers what to do is tricky. They only understand two things, "yes" and "no." When a person writes a program, the computer turns the instructions into billions of "yes" and "no" commands so that the computer can do what the program says. We call these yes-no commands "binary code." We use "ones" to mean "yes" and "zeros" to mean "no." So who do we have to thank for the building blocks of binary code?

**1100000100101001010010**
**0101001110010001110101**

The number one was invented by the Sumerians. They lived about fifty-five hundred years ago (3484 BCE) in Mesopotamia, where the Middle East is today. They used the number one in the very first counting system. Their symbol for one looked like a line with an upside-down triangle on top. The number has been used in math ever since.

Zero took much longer to come about. The Sumerians had a symbol that meant "nothing," but they didn't use it as a number. In 300 BCE, ancient Babylonians, also in Mesopotamia, used

a symbol to show that numbers were different, like the zeros in 10, 100 and 1,000. About six hundred years later, the Mayans in Central America used symbols to stand for zeros in their calendars.

By the 600s, zero had traveled to China and India and had become part of math. An Indian mathematician named Brahmagupta realized that every time you subtract a number from itself, such as four minus four, you always get zero. The idea sounds simple, but it changed math forever.

People in the Middle East learned about Brahmagupta's zero by the year 773. By the 800s, a mathematician named Mohammed Ibn-Musa Khwarizmi used this new zero to do equations. Also by the ninth century, zero had joined the Hindu-Arabic numeral system as the oval shape we use today.

Europeans learned about zero two hundred years later. Famous thinkers such as René Descartes from France, Sir Isaac Newton from England, and Gottfried

Wilhelm Leibniz from Germany used it in their work. Now zero is used in everything from math and physics to engineering and computing. For a number that stands for "nothing," the zero is really something!

# Computer Bites

○ Screens, or monitors, were added to computers around 1964.

○ The first computer mice were made out of wood.

○ The mice were shown to the public by Douglas C. Engelbart in 1968.

○ The first home computer was unveiled in 1975. It was built by Ed Roberts and was called MITS Altair 8800.

○ MicroChess, a chess game, was the first game people could buy for their home computers. Released in 1976, it was the first software package to sell fifty thousand copies.

○ The first laptop like the ones we use today was built by Adam Osborne in 1981. It weighed twenty-four pounds!

○ The Internet as we know it launched in 1991. For the first time, the average person could go online.

○ The first smartphone, Simon, went on sale August 16, 1994. It sold for $1,100 and was about the size of a standard building brick. It had an address book, calculator, calendar, e-mail, sketch pad, clock, to-do list, and—of course—it made phone calls!

# A History of Breaking Boundaries
## Read about some other amazing women in computer technology:

**Ada King**, Countess of Lovelace, who is known as Lady Lovelace, was the first computer programmer—even though she lived one hundred years before the begining of the computer age! In the 1840s, Lovelace worked on the Analytical Engine invented by Charles Babbage. The machine was never built, but it was designed to follow instructions to solve math problems. Lovelace wrote those instructions, including the world's first computer program! She also argued that machines could do so much more than math. Lovelace said machines could process all kinds of information to perform different functions—even compose music. Lovelace's ideas were revolutionary and can be seen in the computers we use today.

**Admiral Grace Hopper** oversaw the programming of UNIVAC I, the world's first commercially available computer. UNIVAC was delivered on June 14, 1951. She later helped create COBOL, a programming language computers still use today. Admiral Hopper is also credited with finding the first "computer bug." It was an actual moth stuck inside the Mark II computer at Harvard!

**Hedy Lamarr** was a famous Hollywood film star. In the early 1940s, she and composer George Antheil patented their "Secret Communications System." It was a way to send messages during wartime. It became the basis for military communications and led the way for cellular phone calls and even Wi-Fi!

**Adele Goldstine** also worked on ENIAC in 1945. She was the first programmer on the project and recruited the rest of the programming team. She wrote the manual on how ENIAC worked and later added a memory system to ENIAC so it could run fifty different programs instead of one.

**Evelyn Boyd Granville** was the second African American woman to earn a PhD in mathematics. In 1956, she accepted a job at NASA and created computer software that tracked the paths of satellites in space. She even worked on the Apollo space program, which landed the first person on the moon!

# Now that you've met the women who launched the computer age, what do you know about them?
## Take this quiz and find out!

1. When was ENIAC built?

a. During World War I      b. During World War II      c. During the Revolutionary War

2. Before there were modern-day computers, the military hired people to figure out complicated math problems. What were the people called?

a. Computers      b. Calculators      c. Mathmeters

3. At the time when ENIAC was built, most women who studied math joined what profession?

a. Researcher      b. Scientist      c. Teacher

4. Why did the military hire women to do math?

a. It was an old tradition.      b. The men were overseas fighting in WWII.

c. Women were better educated.

5. What did the math problems tell the military?

a. How to set their weapons      b. When to attack      c. How much ammunition they had

6. The women programmers learned how to use ENIAC "on the job". What does that mean?

a. They learned it from a book.      b. Someone taught them how.

c. They figured it out as they worked on problems.

7. After ENIAC proved a success, what happened to the women?

a. They were hired to develop a new computer.

b. They were celebrated as pioneers.

c. They were forgotten in their field for nearly forty years.

8. Who rediscovered the programmers of ENIAC?

a. A farm girl from Missouri named Jean Jennings.

b. Engineers John W. Mauchly and John Presper Eckert Jr.

c. A college student named Kathy Kleiman.

Answers: 1.b  2.a  3.c  4.b  5.a  6.c  7.c  8.c